CYCLING
around
NORTHUMBERLAND

Compiled by Arnold Robinson

THE JOHN MERRILL FOUNDATION 2013

Cycling around Series

© Arnold Robinson.

THE JOHN MERRILL FOUNDATION,
32, Holmesdale,
Waltham Cross,
Hertfordshire
EN8 8QY
Tel/Fax 01992 - 762776
email - john@johnmerrillwalkguides.co.uk
www.johnmerrillwalkguides.co.uk

Printed, bound, marketed and distributed by The John Merrill Foundation.

© Text, - Arnold Robinson 2001
© Additional text - John N. Merrill 2001
© Maps and photographs - John Merrill & Arnold Robinson 2001

First Published - March 1997.
This reprint - June 2013.

ISBN 978-1--946404-42-X

British Library Cataloguing-in-Publication Data.
A catalogue record for this book is available from the British Library.

Please note - The maps in this guide are purely illustrative. You are encouraged to use the appropriate 1:50,000 O.S. map.

Meticulous research has been undertaken to ensure that this publication is highly accurate at the time of going to press. The publishers, however, cannot be held responsible for alterations, errors or omissions, but they would welcome notification of such for future editions.

Typeset in AGaramond - bold, italic and plain 10pt, 14pt and 18pt.

Printed by - The John Merrill Foundation
Designed and typset by The John Merrill Foundation

Cover photograph - by Arnold Robinson..

Cover design© The John Merrill Foundation

Printed on paper from a 100% sustainable forest.
The John Merrill Foundation plants sufficient trees through the Woodland Trust to replenish the trees used in its publications.

ABOUT THE AUTHOR

Arnold Robinson has been a dedicated cyclist for sixty years. In that time, he has cycled in every county in England and Wales, each region of Scotland, in Ireland and Europe. He first cycled around Cotswolds in 1935 and during subsequent years, has cycled for many hundreds of miles in the area exploring the delightful byroads, searching out the charming villages and beautiful countryside. He has ridden and recroded each of the rides in this guide, some of them on several occasions.

After spending most of his childhood in Derbyshire and Nottinghamshire, in 1939 he moved to Sheffield to join the Police Force. When he retired in 1969, he held the rank of Detective Chief Superintendent and was head of the Criminal Investigation Department of Sheffield and Rotherham. After a spell as Police Consultant to Yorkshire Television and in industrial security, he became a freelance writer, broadcaster and photographer on outdoor activities but mainly cycling.

He regularly contributes articles and photographs to cycling magazines and is the author of a series of regional cycling guides covering the whole of Britain. He was also a major contributor of routes for 'Cyclists' Britain' published in 1985 by Ordnance Survey/Pan Books and contributed routes to the new Marks & Spencer/AA Cycling guide, recently published.

His first of nearly two hundred broadcasts on cycling was made In 1939. For five years he was the presenter of BBC Radio Sheffield's cycling programme 'On your Bike'.

3

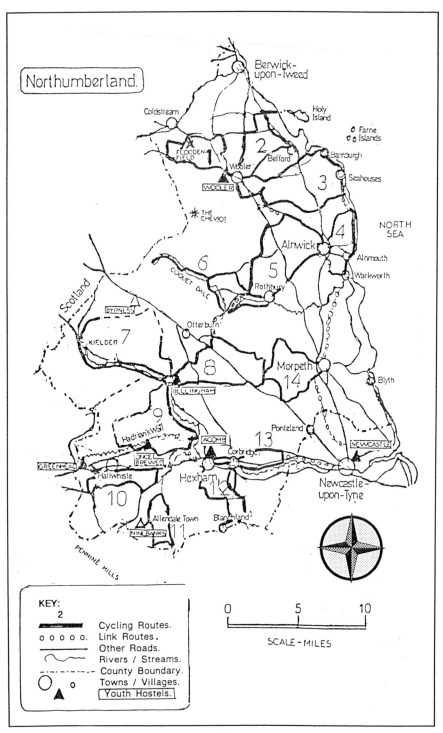

Northumberland.

Berwick-upon-Tweed

Coldstream

Holy Island

Farne Islands

FLODDEN FIELD

Wooler

Belford

Bamburgh

WOOLER

Seahouses

THE CHEVIOT

Alnwick

NORTH SEA

Alnmouth

Warkworth

Scotland

COQUET DALE

Rothbury

BYRNESS

Otterburn

KIELDER

HADRIAN'S WALL

ACOMB

Morpeth

Blyth

BELLINGHAM

Ponteland

Corbridge

NEWCASTLE

GREENHEAD

ONCE BREWED

Haltwhistle

Hexham

Newcastle-upon-Tyne

Allendale Town

Blanchland

NINE BANKS

PENNINE HILLS

KEY:
2
━━━━ Cycling Routes.
o o o o o. Link Routes.
──── Other Roads.
∿∿∿ Rivers / Streams.
─·─·─· County Boundary.
◯ ▲ o Towns / Villages.
Youth Hostels.

SCALE - MILES
0   5   10

4

Contents

Key to ROUTE MAPS:

Cycling Routes.

Alternative Cycling Routes.

Main Roads.

Other Roads.

Unsurfaced roads and tracks.

Railways.

Rivers/Streams.

Lakes/Reservoirs.

Built up areas.

Towns/Villages.

Church.

Youth Hostel.

Camp Site.

Places of interest.

Summit.

Viewpoint.

KEY TO ABBREVIATIONS in ITINERARIES:

Inf: Tourist Information Office.
EC   Early Closing Day.
MD   Market Day.
BR: British Railway Passenger Station.
B&B   Bed & Breakfast accomodation.
YH   Youth Hostel.
SC   Self catering.
Cafe   Cafe or Restaurant.
PM   Pub Meals.
Sh   Shops supplying food.
T: Toilets.
Cmg: Camp Sites.
Cvg: Caravan sites.
Sp: Signpost.
TR: Traffic island.
TL: Traffic lights.

INTRODUCTION

Since Newcastle-upon-Tyne and its immediate environs were transferred by the local authority boundary changes to the 'new county' of Tyne & Wear, Northumberland is almost entirely a rural area - and what a delightful rural area it is.

It is an awkward shape stretching for over 70 miles from the high Pennines in the remote south west corner of the county in a north easterly direction along the Scottish border to the coast beyond Berwick-upon-Tweed. Although it is unlikely to be considered by many cyclists for a summer tour, it has some varied and very beautiful scenery, a dramatic coastline, interesting castles, many square miles of forest, some delightful river valleys and - most important - many miles of quiet cycling byroads even at the height of the holiday season. There are even some comparatively mild off highway routes. Very few of the suggested routes involve really strenuous hill climbs.

The only roads which cyclists are advised to avoid are the A1 which runs up the eastern edge of the county from Newcastle-upon-Tyne to Berwick-upon-Tweed; the A697 which leaves the A1 north of Morpeth and cuts across country to Wooler and Coldstream; the A68 Carter Bar road from Corbridge to Jedbergh and its connecting link from Newcastle the A696, and the A69 through the Tyne Valley. The B6318, the Military Road from Newcastle-upon-Tyne to Greenhead carries more traffic than its status may suggest although sections of this may have to be used to visit some of the attractions relating to the Roman Wall and other antiquities.

My first visit to Northumberland was in 1951 on a tandem tour which took me from Haltwhistle by way of Hexham, Bellingham, Rothbury and Coquetdale, Alnwick, the coast through Seahouses to Bamburgh and back to Newcastle-upon-Tyne. It was a wonderful trip when everything was 'new'. I have returned on many occasions always discovering fresh delights. For this quide, I have selected my favourite rides which present the county's many different faces; its most attractive villages and byways and places of interest.

The Routes.

The routes have been designed, so far as is practicable, to follow quiet byways so avoiding the heavy traffic which bedevils the main roads on summer weekends and during holiday periods. By keeping to the byways, it is possible to ride for long periods seeing few motor vehicles.

East of the rides could form the basis for a 'day ride' or by using the link routes indicated on the map on page 4, be combined into an on-going tour.

7

Some of the rides have optional extensions or diversions (see Notes at the foot of the Itineraries). Alternatively, the mileage might be reduced by using one or more of the alternative routes indicated on the maps.

Cyclists who are adept at planning their own routes will find the touring information useful when looking for a 'new' route or a variation of past tours.

The Towns.

Cyclists invariably try to avoid busy towns when planning their routes, but there are no cities and the towns in Northumberland - Hexham, Haltwhistle, Morpeth, Alnwick and Berwick-upon-Tweed - do not present any problems. For Touring Information and other details of the various towns visited on the Rides see the Route Itineraries.

The Villages.

The rides have been planned to allow visits to the most picturesque and interesting villages in the county and time should be allowed to visit these.

Ride No. 1: Ford Etal, Branxton.
Ride No. 2. Holy Island.
Ride No. 3. Chillingham, Beadnell Harbour, Bamburgh.
Ride No. 4. Dunstan, Craster, Warkworth.
Ride No. 5 Whittingham, Rothbury, Edingham.
Ride No. 6. Bellingham, Holystone, Alwinton.
Ride No. 7. Falstone, Keilder.
Ride No. 8. Elsdon, Cambo, Kirkwhelpington.
Ride No. 9. Wark, Simonsburn.
Ride No.10. Beltingham.
Ride No.11. Allendale Town and Allenheads.
Ride No.12. Blanchland.
Ride No.13. Bywell, Ovingham, Wylam.
Ride No.14. Belsay, Netherwhitton.

Places of Interest.

The rides also allow for visits to places of historical interest, castles, abbeys, churches etc.

Flodden Field (Ride No.1.)
Holy Island and Lindisfarne Castle (Ride No.2).
Ross Castle, Chillingham Park, Seahouses and Bamburgh (Ride No.3).
Alnwick, Craster and Warkworth (Ride No.4).
Rothbury (Ride No.5).
Holystone and Coquet Dale (Ride No.6).
Bellingham, the North Tyne valley and Keilder Water (Ride No.7).
Elsdon and Wallington Hall (Ride No.8).

8

Wark Forest, Hadrian's Wall and Chesters and other Museums (Ride No.9).
The South Tyne valley (Ride No.10).
Allendale Town and the Allen valleys (Ride No.11).
Hexham, Blanchland and the Derwent Reservoir (Ride No.12).
Corbridge and the Tyne Valley (Ride No.13).
Morpeth, Bolam Lake, the Font and Wansbeck valleys. (Ride No.14).

Accommodation.
Details of accommodation may be obtained from the various Tourist Information Offices (see below) The CTC Handbook also lists details of recommended Bed & Breakfast accommodation.

Details of the Youth Hostels in Northumberland are given in the itineraries and on pages 65 - 67.

Camp Sites.
The location of Camp Sites is shown in the Information Section of the Route Itineraries and on the Route Maps.

Tourist Information.
There are Tourist Information Offices at Wooler, Seahouses, Alnwick, Bellingham, Rothbury, Morpeth, Hexham and Keilder most of which operate a Book-a-Bed Service.

Where to Eat.
The location of cafes and pubs providing meals are shown in the itineraries but on routes through the more remote areas, it is advisable to carry emergency supplies of food and drink.

Cycle Repairers.
Approved cycle repairers who carry a stock of spares and accessories and can also carry out emergency repairs are available in Bellingham, Keilder Water and Rothbury.

Maps.
The route maps are sufficiently detailed within the scope of the scale to enable the Itinerary to be followed without difficulty but greater details will be found on the Ordnance Survey Landranger Sheets No. 75, 80, 81, 87 and 88.

Acknowledgement.
I am indebted to Daphne Houghton and Heather Evans of the Cyclists' Touring Club's Northumberland District Association for assistance in checking and updating my notes. Their 'local' knowledge has been invaluable.

Ride No. 1
From Wooler - Etal and Flodden Field
- 30 miles

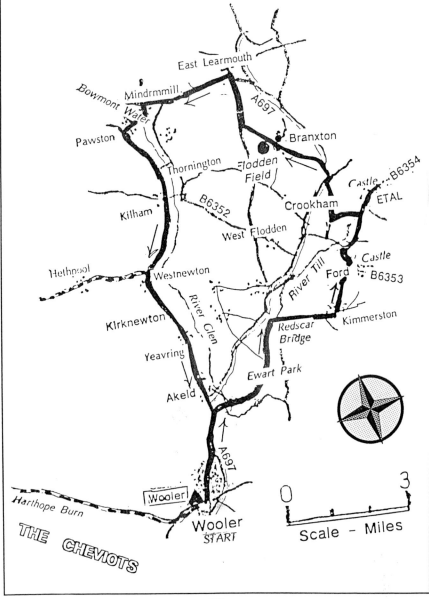

Ride No. 1
From WOOLER:
ETAL and FLODDEN
FIELD. - 30 Miles.

This ride follows byroads in the north west corner of the county closely follows the River Till to FORD and ETAL, both very pleasant and interesting villages. It then turns westwards through the picturesque village of BRANXTON to the site of the Battle of Flodden Field. At East Yearmouth when close to the Scottish border the route turns south through open country before joining the valley of the Bowmont Water which later becomes the River Glen. For the student of ancient history, there is much to explore around Kirknewton and Yeavering.

Gradients: For the most part, the ride is gently undulating with no strenuous climbs. **MAPS.** Ordnance Survey Sheets 74 and 75.

Miles.	Places and route itinerary.	Information and Points of Interest.
	WOOLER. From centre, turn westwards along Main Street; turn L along Burnhouse Road, in one-mile at T junc (A697); turn L and then turn R on byroad continue past:	EC: Thurs. Inf. B&B. YH. Sh. C. Cmg. Cvg. Picturesque location below northern slopes of CHEVIOT HILLS. Good centre for cycling around the north west corner of the county. Site (motte) of Norman Castle. Harthope Valley. Picturesque diversion into Cheviots, 10 miles return.
3.5	**EWART PARK.** continue ahead and in 2m turn R across REDSCAR Bridge, continue to:	18 cent. house now derelict. C at Millfield, half-mile W of Redscar Bridge.
3.0	**KIMMERSTON.** Turn L and continue to:	Hamlet farms. (2m from Roughling Linn (see Ride No.2).
1.5	**FORD.** At T junc (B6352) turn L; in half-mile continue straight ahead (see note a) on B6354 to:	EC: Wed. C. at PO. Model village. Castle, rebuilt 18 cent and 19 cent. but contains two 13 cent towers. Not open to public. Paintings in former school. Church: 13 cent. Altered 19 cent. Bell turrett.

Miles.	Places and route itinerary.	Information and Points of
2.0	**ETAL** Retrace route and turn R across bridge; continue on byroad and at T junc (B6353) turn R; continue to:	EC: Tues. C at PO. Picturesque thatched cottages and pub. Remains of 14 cent castle. 18 cent Manor House - woodland gardens. River Till - salmon leap. Heatherslaw working water corn mill. Cafe. 15 inch gauge stream beteween Heatherslaw and Etal.
2.5	**CROOKHAM.** At T junc (A697) turn R and in 200 yds turn L on byroad to:	Small rural village.
1.5	**BRANXTON.** At end of village, continue ahead on minor road to:	Picturesque village. 'Stone Jungle' in garden full of animals and other statues.
0.5	**Site of FLODDEN FIELD.** Continue ahead to T junc and turn R (see note b) on byroad to:	Site of Battle between English and Scots in 1513 when James IV and 3,000 of his army were killed a catastrophy for Scotland. Monument in field to L of road.
2.0	**EAST LEARMOUTH.** Turn L and continue to:	Small border village.
2.5	**MINDRUMMIL.** At X rds turn L (B6352) and in 200 yds turn R on byroad to:	Hamlet at cross roads, junction of roads to Wooler, Kelso and Kirk Yetholm.
1.0	**PAWSTON.** At T junc turn L and in 2m at:	Small farming village.
2.0	**KILHAM.** Continue straight ahead on B6351 to:	Hamlet here join B6351. Northern slopes of Cheviots on R.
2.0	**WESTNEWTON.** (see note c) Continue ahead through:	Farming hamlet at foot of College valley which runs deep into Cheviot Hills.

Miles	Places and route itinerary.	Information and Points of Interest.
0.5	**KIRKNEWTON.** Continue through:	Small peaceful village in beautiful situation. Church; St. Gregory. 19 cent. but retains primitive tunnel vaulted chancel and south transept. Graves of airmen killed in 1939-45 war flying from nearby Millfield airfield.
1.5	**YEAVERING.** Continue to:	Gefrin monument to L of road. Site of 7 cent palace discovered from air as crop marks in 1949. Forts and ancient settlements on surrounding hilltops. Yeavering Bell is largest and most important iron age 'town' in the county. Battle Stone, W of Yeavering on R of road. 10ft. high.
1.5	**AKELD.** At T junc. turn R (A697) and in 1.5m turn R on byroad into:	Village at road junction. Bastle house. Several hill forts in vicinity.
2.5	**WOOLER.**	

NOTES:

(a) The diversion to ETAL may be omitted and a direct route taken from FORD to CROOKHAM via the B6353, reducing the distance by two miles. (See map).

(b) The diversion through EAST LEARMOUTH and PAWSTON might be omitted and a direct route taken via THORNINGTON to KILHAM reducing the distance by 3 miles. (See map).

(c) From WEST NEWTON, there is an optional and strenuous diversion to HETHPOOL and through a secluded Chilterns valley. (Peel Tower). (See map).

Ride No. 2
From Wooler:
Doddington and Holy Island - 41.5 miles

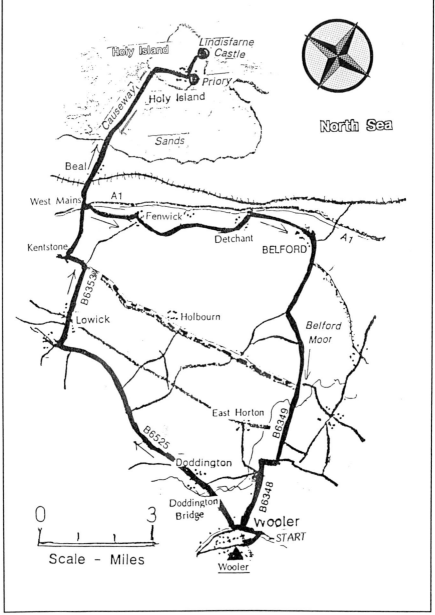

Ride No. 2
From Wooler:
DODDINGTON and
HOLY ISLAND.
- 41.5 Miles.

The highlight of this ride is a visit to Lindisfarne Priory and Castle on Holy Island. The castle stands on a rock on the coast but - and this is most important - the island can only be reached at low tide as the approach is across a causeway which is covered by the tide for several hours each day. Before embarking on the trip, make certain that there is time to get back to the mainland before the next high tide which lasts for six hours. The return via BELFORD would normally involve five miles along the A1 but this can be avoided by turning on to a parallel byway.
A history of Holy Island and Lindisfarne is described in Ward Lock's guide *'Complete NORTHUMBRIA'*.

GRADIENTS: Although not a strenuous ride, there are several climbs (1) after leaving DODDINGTON (2) for several miles after leaving BELFORD.

MAPS - Ordnance Survey Landranger Sheet 75

Miles.	Places and route itinerary.	Information and Points of Interest.
	WOOLER. From town centre, descend Church Street to T junc (A697) and turn L; in 400 yds turn R on B6525; cross Doddington Bridge and continue into:	See Ride No.1. River Till.
3.5	**DODDINGTON.** Continue through village and climb for one mile then continue through open country; after sharp R turn at Barmoor, continue ahead on B6353 into:	Remains of prehistoric hill fort above. village to east. Castle Tower, c.1584 in farmyard. Small rural village in Till valley. Many cup and ring marked rocks to east and south east. The best and most accesible are at Roughling Linn between Kinnerston (Ride No.1) and Lowick. Watch House for Body Snatchers (1856).

15

Miles.	Places and route itinerary.	Information and Points of
5.5	**LOWICK.** At X rds in 1.5 miles, turn L and in half mile turn R on narrow byroad through:	Small village.
2.5	**KENTSTONE.** Continue to X rds (junc A1) (see note a) and continue ahead; in half-mile cross level crossing into:	Farming hamlet. Look out for NO-TICE re times of High Tide when Causeway is closed. Main east coast line. Pub at A1 junction.
2.0	**BEAL.** Continue ahead and descend to:	EC: Thurs. Small village on approach to HOLY ISLAND.
1.0	**HOLY ISLAND CAUSEWAY.** Continue ahead to.	Check notice re times of High Tides. Sea Birds.
3.5	**HOLY ISLAND. Village.** Continue through village and turn L on narrow byroad to:	Inf. B&B. Sh. PM. C. Extensive remains of Norman priory 7 cent. Celtic monastry of St.Aidan and St.Cuthbert. Attractive ancient village Market Cross. Church - St. Mary's.
1.0	**LINDISFARNE CASTLE.** Retrace route through village and across CAUSEWAY then continue through:	16 cent. fort. on steep outcrop. NT. Converted to a remarkable romantic house in 1903 by Sir. Edward Lutyens. Lime kilns near castle in good condition. Traditionally lived in upturned boats by the harbour. Some remain as stores.
5.5	**BEAL.** Continue to X rds (junc A1) and turn L (see note a); in 200 yds turn R on byroad; in 1.5m at T junc (B5353) turn L into:	
3.0	**FENWICK.** Turn R on byroad; continue through open country to:	Small village lying aside from A1. Manor House was a YH 1946-54.
3.0	**DETCHANT.** Turn L in village to T junc (old A1) and turn R through:	

Miles	Places and route itinerary.	Information and Points of Interest.
1.0	**MIDDLETON.** Continue ahead and after short climb descend into:	Once on busy A1 but now on quiet side road.
1.0	**BELFORD.** Turn R (B6349) and start steady climb to BELFORD MOOR; continue climbing across LYHAM MOOR and then descend LYHAM HILL; continue through;	EC. Thurs. MD: Tues. B&B Sh. Cafe. Large village formerly on A1 but now bypassed.
4.0	**WEST LYHAM.** Continue ahead and cross bridge (River Till) and then climb to T junc. turn R (B6348) and cross Wooler Water and A697; continue ahead up Church Street to Main Street of:	Cross roads in open country. Fowberry Tower in woods on L over bridge.
5.0	**WOOLER.**	

NOTES:
(a) There is an alternative route for the return ride between BEAL and WEST LYHAM through open country via Holborn. (See map).

Lindisfarne Castle stands on a rock which rises above the sandy beach of Holy Island.

17

Ride No. 3
From Wooler:
Seahouses and Bamburgh - 46 miles

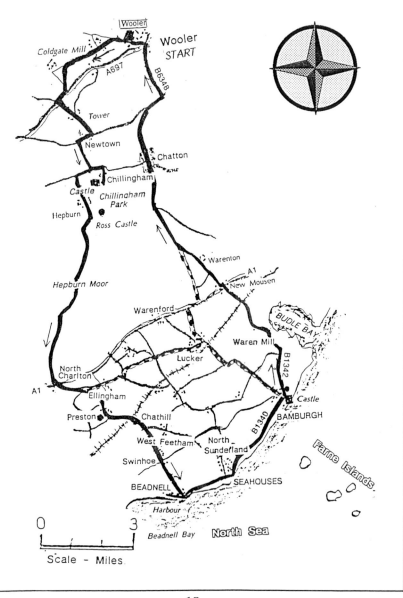

Wooler

Wooler
START

Coldgate Mill

A697

B6348

Tower

Newtown

Chatton

Chillingham

Castle
Chillingham
Park

Hepburn

Ross Castle

Warenton

A1

New Mousen

Hepburn Moor

Warenford

BUDLE BAY

Waren Mill

B1342

Lucker

North
Charlton

A1

Ellingham

Castle

BAMBURGH

Preston

Chathill

B1340

West Feetham

North
Sundefland

Fame Islands

Swinhoe

BEADNELL

SEAHOUSES

Harbour

0   3

Beadnell Bay   North Sea

Scale - Miles

18

Ride No. 3
From Wooler:
SEAHOUSES and
BAMBURGH
- 46 miles

This ride first follows a byways route to CHILLINGHAM, home of a herd of wild white cattle and then climbs to HEPBURN MOOR. After crossing the A1 at NORTH CHARLTON there are more byroads to the coast at BEADNELL which has an attractive harbour. For several miles the route then follows the coast through SEAHOUSES to BAMBURGH whose castle rises majestically above a sandy beach. From BAMBURGH, there is a choice of ways (see map) but with very little to choose between them either by gradients or scenically. After climbing to Chatton Moor, the route descends and crosses the River Till into the village of CHATTON. The ride might be divided into two halves: (a) from WOOLER around CHILLINGHAM and CHATTON and (b) starting from BEADNELL to SEAHOUSES or BAMBURGH (See map).

Gradients: There is a strenuous climb from the village of HEPBURN after which riding is very easy but there are some gradual climbs on the return.

Maps - Ordnance Survey Landranger Sheet No. 75

Miles.	Places and route itinerary.	Information and Points of Interest.
	WOOLER. From Town centre turn R up Cheviot Street and climb past entrance to Youth Hostel; in half-mile fork L and in 2m descend to ford at:	See Ride No.1.
2.5	**COLDGATE MILL.** Continue ahead and in half-mile turn L; descend and at next junction, again turn L to T junc (A697); turn R and in half-mile turn L on byroad; in half-mile turn L over bridge past:	Pleasant location at foot of Happy Valley. Busy main road, care when crossing. C - Restaurant at old railway station on A697 just past turn.

Miles.	Places and route itinerary.	Information and Points of
2.0	**LILBURN TOWER.** In one-mile fork R through:	19 cent. mansion (not visible from road). Pleasant situation. Ruined tower in large wooded grounds occasionally open to public.
1.5	**NEWTOWN.** Turn L and in one-mile turn L: in half-mile turn R into:	Farming hamlet. Unusual gateway at entrance to Chillingham Castle.
2.0	**CHILLINGHAM.** Retrace route and turn L: continue past gates to Castle and in half-mile turn L to:	Picturesque estate village. Interesting church. Splendid castle of many periods, 14c-18c. Associated with Edward I. Open to public. Wild white cattle roam in park, can be visited.
2.0	**HEPBURN.** Climb very steeply to open moor; continue to:	Small village below moor. Track on L at summit to ROSS CASTLE (400 yds). Hill Fort (NT) with spectacular views.
7.5	**NORTH CHARLTON.** At T junc (A1) turn L and immediately turn R on byroad; in one-mile at X rds, turn R to:	Small hamlet. Care when crossing main road.
2.5	**PRESTON.** At T junc. turn L to:	Pele Tower, 14 cent.
1.0	**CHATHILL.** Cross level crossing and continue ahead through:	Main east coast line.
2.0	**SWINHOE.** At X rds continue straight ahead on B1340 (sp Beadnell) and in one-mile turn R on narrow byroad (sp Beadnell village) into:	Small farming hamlet. Here join main coastal route from ALNWICK.
1.5	**BEADNELL.** Continue through village to T junc. and turn R to:	Sh. Holiday resort. Small coastal village.

Miles	Places and route itinerary.	Information and Points of Interest.
0.5	**BEADNELL HARBOUR.** Retrace route and continue straight ahead (B1340) past Golf Course:	B&B. Cvg. Cmg. Small fishing village with picturesque harbour. 18 cent. lime kilns. NT. Sandy beach.
3.0	**SEAHOUSES.** Turn R along Main Street and continue ahead to Harbour; then turn L and again turn L to return to junc. with B1340; turn R along coast road and continue to:	EC: Wed. Inf. B&B. Sh. Cvg. C. PM. Harbour - boats to Farne Islands (NT) breeding place for grey seals and sea birds. View of Farne Islands. Sand dunes.
3.0	**BAMBURGH.** At top of green, fork R (sp B1342 Waren Mill); continue along shore of BUDLE BAY and cross bridge into:	EC: Wed. B&B. Sh. C. PM. Cvg. Cmg. Small peaceful resort with 19 cent. cottages alongside triangular wooded green. Magnificent castle on precipitous outcrop dominates village and coast. Norman keep. Largely rebuilt in 18-19 cent. Open to public daily in summer. St. Andrew's Church: crypt, Grace Darling tomb. Grace Darling Museum contains cobble on which she sailed and performed rescue. Sandy beach.
2.5	**WAREN MILL.** Turn L B1342 (sp Belford); climb for half-mile and turn R; in half-mile turn L (sp Trunk Road) on byroad; cross railway bridge and continue to T junc (A1); turn L to:	Small village at head of BUDLE BAY. Tidal sands, good for bird watching. Cvg. cmg. Quiet country byroad.
2.5	**NEW MOUSEN.** In 300 yds turn R (sp Old Mousen) on byroad; climb for half-mile and turn R (sp Chatton); climb through:	Care when turning.
1.5	**WARENTON.** Climb to T junc (B6348) and turn R; gradually descend then cross bridge (River Till) into:	Small farming village. Extensive views. Cup and ring rocks R of road. (One-mile east of bridge and 500 yds (from road).
3.5	**CHATTON.** Continue ahead and in 2m at T junc. turn R then continue ahead descend; cross bridge (Wooler Water) and A697 then continue ahead up Church Street into:	Pleasant agricultural village. Church has belfry. Fowberry Tower on right.
5.0	**WOOLER.**	

Ride No. 4
From Alnwick:
Craster and Warkworth - 31 miles

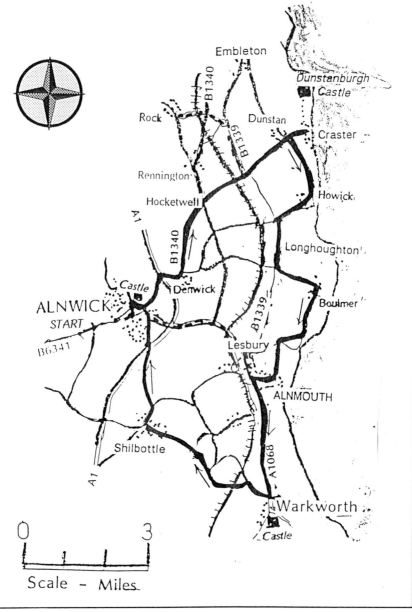

Scale - Miles

Ride No. 4
From ALNWICK:
CRASTER AND
WARKWORTH.
- 31 Miles.

The route first runs out to the coast at CRASTER, a quaint fishing village from where there is an optional walk along the cliffs to the impressive ruins of Dunstanburgh Castle. From CRASTER, the route follows byroads through some small coastal villages to ALNMOUTH, a quiet resort on its bay, A few miles of main road - the A1068 - then have to be followed to WARKWORTH, an attractive old village which has an impressive castle. The coast from ALNWOUTH north to BERWICK-upon-TWEED has been designated as an area of outstanding natural beauty.

Gradients: The route is mainly undulating with no really strenuous climbs.
Maps - Ordnance Survey Landranger Sheet No. 81.

Miles.	Places and route itinerary.	Information and Points of Interest.
	ALNWICK. From Market Place, turn east along Bondgate Within; continue through arch and in 200 yds at Tenantry Column; fork L (Denwick Road) (B1340) descend to bridge (River Aln); climb; cross bridge (A1) and continue into:	EC: Wed. MD: Sat. Inf. B&B, C. PM. Cvg. Cmg. Cyc. Touring centre. Ancient and picturesque town centre which has grown up around Medieval Castle seat of Dukes of Northumberland. Tenantry Column, 1816, known as 'Farmer's Folly'. Cross in Market Place. Pottergate Tower and Hotspur Gate. Castle approach from Bailiff Gate by 14 cent barbican with figures of soldiers on roof. Keep from Norman times has been altered many times, now reflects mid 19 cent. taste of the 4th Duke. A1 once passed through town centre but is now diverted along bypass to east. Church of St. Michael, much restored. Fine view of castle from bridge.
1.5	DENWICK. Turn L and then fork L (B1340); and continue for 2m to:	Small village.

Miles.	Places and route itinerary.	Information and Points of
2.0	HOCKETWELL. Turn R (see note a) and imm. turn L on byroad; cross railway at level crossing and at X rds (junc B1339) continue str. ahead on byroad; at next X rds continue straight ahead and descend to T junc. and turn R; descend into:	Road junction. Byroad through open country. Byroad on left into DUNSTAN village. Craster Tower on right. Dunstan Hall, 15 cent.
3.5	CRASTER. (See note b). Retrace route and turn L; then at X rds. turn L and in 1.5 miles turn R into:	Inf. Sh. C. PM. Cvg. Cmg. Quaint fishing village famous for oak smoked kippers. Fine cliff scenery. Fine coastal scenery approaching HOWICK.
2.5	HOWICK. (See note c) Continue to T junc. and turn R; descend into wooded valley and in 1m join B1339; continue ahead and at T junc. turn L to:	Small village standing back from cliffs. Pleasant walk along coast to beach at Howick Haven. Extensive wooded grounds to Hall, 18 cent (Rebuilt 1926 after fire). Open to public in summer.
2.5	LONGHOUGHTON. At X rds turn L to:	Sh. C. Agricultural village. Church has prominent tower. Ratcheugh Crag (2m west) has extensive views.
1.5	BOULMER. Turn R along coast road and in 2m turn L on byroad to:	Small farming village on cliffs. Once a smuggling centre.
3.5	ALNMOUTH. Continue through village to end; then retrace route to TR, turn L (B1338); in one mile at TR, turn L (A1068) (see note d); in 3m descend to bridge (River Coquet) and continue into:	EC: Wed. BR. Sh. C. Quiet resort with extensive sands. Formerly a seaport. Has ancient golf course. A terrible storm in 1806 changed course of River Aln and left harbour on south side.
	.	

Miles	Places and route itinerary.	Information and Points of Interest.
4.0	**WARKWORTH.** Retrace route and immediately after crossing bridge, turn L on byroad; continue to:	EC: Thurs. B&B. Sh. C. PM. Village is entered over modern bridge which replaced nearby 14 cent bridge. River Coquet makes hairpin loop around village. Main street climbs to impressive ruins of castle. 13 and 14 cent. St. Laurence's Church: Norman. Cross Hermitage up River from Castle. Elaborate cave dwelling and 14 cent. chapel. Access by ferry
11.0	**HOUNDEAN MILL.** Cross railway and continue on winding byroad turning L at two T junctions to:	Quiet byroad.
3.0	**SHILBOTTLE.** At church turn R (sp Alnwick) in half-mile turn L (sp Alnwick); in 1.5m pass under bridge (A1) and turn R; rejoin outward route at Tenantry Column and continue into:	Formerly a colliery village on high ground. Good views.
6.0	**ALNWICK.**	

NOTES:

(a) At the road junction at HOCKETWELL, the B1340 continues to REMINGTON from where a byroad leads to ROCK, (Picturesque cottages). Hall was formerly a Youth Hostel but is now privately owned.

(b) From CRASTER, there is an interesting walk (3 miles return) along the cliffs to the ruins of DUNSTANBURGH CASTLE. Fine cliff scenery.

(c) From HOLWICK Sea Houses, there is a public byway along the cliffs to BOULMER with splendid sea views. This is not all rideable but is shorter than the road.

(d) From ALNMOUTH, there is a more direct route to ALNWICK along the A1068 but this omits WARKWORTH.

Ride No. 5
From Alnwick:
Powbnurn and Rothbury - 40.5 miles
Optional extension - Beamish Valley

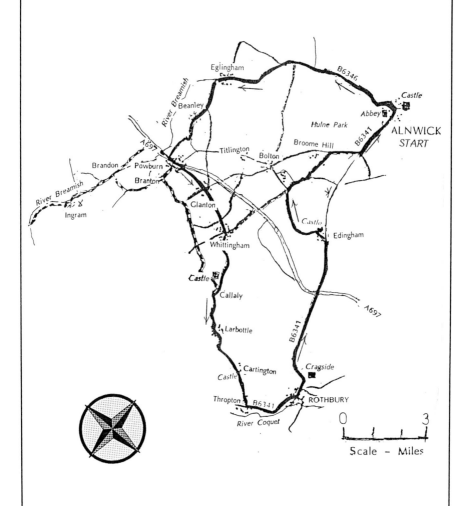

Ride No. 5
From ALNWICK:
POWBURN and
ROTHBURY
- 40.5 Miles.
Optional extension: BEAMISH VALLEY.

The route for this ride follows quiet byroads though open countryside to the many small villages to the west and south west of ALNWICK. Although there are no high spots, the route runs through some quiet countryside ideal for leisurely cycling finally leading to the village of ROTHBURY in a beautiful situation in the COQUET VALLEY. The return across open moorland is less interesting.

The ride may conveniently be divided into two halves. From POWBURN, there is an optional extension into the delightful BREAMISH VALLEY (see map) and from WHITTINGHAM, turning back to ALNWICK. The remainder of the main route could then form the basis for another ride from ALNWICK. (See Notes and Map).

Gradients: This is a fairly hilly ride, the more strenuous climbs being **(a)** after leaving ALNWICK on the B6346; **(b)** after POWBURN; **(c)** after WHITTINGHAM; **(d)** between LORBOTTLE and CARTINGTON; **(d)** on the B6341 after ROTHLEY, and **(e)** Broome Hill; after ROTHBURY. The last few miles along the BREAMISH VALLEY which is a cul-de-sac involve a very steep climb.
Map - Ordnance Survey Landranger Sheet No. 81

Miles.	Places and route itinerary.	Information and Points of Interest.
	ALNWICK. From Market Place, turn L along Narrowgate and in 250 yds turn L into Bailiff Cross Gate and continue along Cannon Gate (B6346); descend and cross bridge (River Aln); climb and then continue through open country to:	See Ride No.4. Abbey gatehouse (ruins) on L Hulne Priory on L stands in large park. 13 cent. well preserved. Cycling not permitted in park.
7.5	**EGLINGHAM.** At X rds turn L on byroad and in 1m fork R through:	Sh. PM. Picturesque village on road from Alnwick to Wooler. Church - St. Maurice. Hall - 18th cent.

Miles.	Places and route itinerary.	Information and Points of
2.0	**BEANLEY.** In half-mile turn R and after short descent, continue to T junc (A697); turn L into:	Small farming hamlet.
2.5	**POWBURN.** Continue through village and when main road bends to L; fork R on byroad; (see notes a and b); climb to:	Sh. Cafe. Small village on busy road from MORPETH to SCOTLAND via Wooler.
1.5	**GLANTON.** Turn L into village and then turn R on byroad to:	Sh. PM. Small village standing aside fom A697. Views.
2.0	**WHITTINGHAM.** Take second turn R over bridge on byroad; climb for one-mile and continue to:	Sh. PM. Picturesque village in open valley of upper reaches of River Aln. Church, Anglo-Saxon but much rebuilt, Pele Tower, now almshouses.
2.5	**CALLALY.** Continue ahead past:	Castle in parkland on R. Large house incorporating medieval tower. divided into Flats. Hill fort to east is ironage and later.
1.5	**LORBOTTLE HALL.** and in 1m turn L on byroad; climb steeply to:	Quiet byroad with extensive views.
2.5	**CARTINGTON.** Descend steeply at first to:	Castle remains incorporated into large house. View on R of Upper Coquet Dale and Cheviot Hills.
1.5	**THROPTON.** At T junc (B62341) at east end of village, turn L and continue through COQUET DALE into:	Sh. PM. Small straggling village on north side of Upper Coquet Dale. View of Simonside to south.

28

Miles	Places and route itinerary.	Information and Points of Interest.
1.5	**ROTHBURY.** Continue ahead and in half-mile turn L (B6341), climb past gates to CRAGSIDE; climb steeply at times and continue across open moorland to:	EC: Wed. MD. Alt Mon. Inf. B&B. Sh. C. Cvg. Cmg. Attractive small town with tree lined main street at two levels. Pleasant riverside. Touring centre. CRADSIDE: (NT). Splendid hillside estate. woods, lakes, rocks, and wild gardens. First house in world to be lit by Hydro-electricity. Road now climbs through wooded valley to open moorland.
4.0	**A697 - Cross Roads.** Continue straight ahead and in 2m turn L (see note b) into:	Junction of Morpeth - Wooler and Alnwick - Rothbury roads.
2.5	**EDLINGHAM.** Climb through village and in 2.5 miles at X rds, turn R; descend and in one-mile bear L on minor road then climb, steeply at times up:	Cvg. Cmg. Small village of stone cottages in valley below moors. Church, St. John-the-Baptist, 12 cent. Norman doorway, eight sided font. Village once had a station on the Alnwick Coldstream branch line but now only a bridge and a tunnel remain. Castle (13 cent and later) in ruins in care of English Heritage.
4.0	**BROOME HILL.** Continue ahead and in 1.5m at T junc (B6341), turn L and descend to:	
5.5	ALNWICK:	

NOTES:
(a) From POWBURN, there is an optional extension of the ride through Brandon and Ingram (inf. Cafe. Cmg) into the BREAMISH VALLEY. This is a delightful and worth while diversion (Ten miles return from POWBURN) (See map).
(b) From POWBURN, there is an alternative route to CALLALY along a quiet country byroad through BRANTON (see map). Distance approx the same.
(c) The ride may be divided into two halves by turning left in WHITTINGHAM and joining the main route at cross roads north of EDLINGHAM (see map) Distance 22 miles. The southern half of the ride to ROTHBURY might then be resumed at WHITTINGHAM as a separate ride.

Ride No. 6
From Rothbury:
Upper Coquet Valley - 48 miles

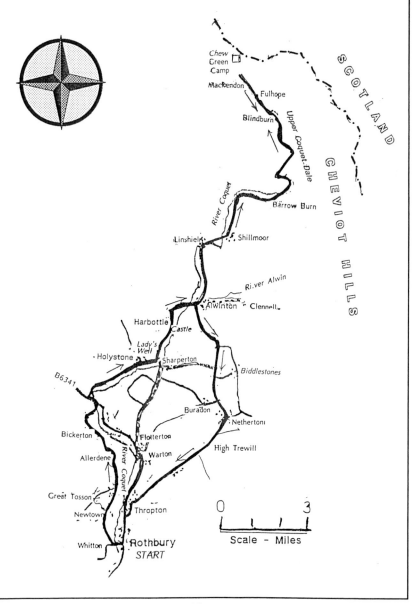

Ride No. 6
From ROTHBURY:
UPPER COQUET
VALLEY
- 48 Miles.

One of the most remote and secluded valleys in the north of England is Coquet Dale which buries its head deep in the Cheviot Hills. From Rothbury the 'capital' of the dale, it is a long ride to Mackendon, the last farm in the valley. This is only one mile from the Scottish border and the site of the Roman Station at CHEW GREEN. The road keeps close to the river which it crosses frequently as they share the narrow gap between steep hillsides. The mileage might be reduced by turning back at Alwinton or any other point in the valley. There are no facilities for refreshments in the Upper Dale so it is advisable to carry food and drink.

GRADIENTS: Variable. From an altitude of 300 ft at ROTHBURY, the road climbs to 1250 feet at MACKENDON but the return is sheer delight with long stretches of free-wheeling.

Maps - Ordnance Survey Landranger Sheets Nos. 80 and 81.

Miles.	Places and route itinerary.	Information and Points of Interest.
	ROTHBURY. From Main Street turn on to B6342; cross bridge (River Coquet) and immediately turn R on byroad; climb steeply into:	See Ride No. 5.
1.0	**WHITTON.** Turn R and continue along hillside through:	Cvg. Cmg. Whitton Tower, 14 cent. Pele tower, formerly rectory. Views of valley ahead.
1.5	**NEWTOWN.** Turn R and in half-mile bear R through:	Faming hamlet. Fine views. Quiet country byroad.
1.0	**ALLERDENE.** Bend L and continue along lower slopes of TODDON HILL; continue through:	Hamlet below slopes of Tosson Hill. Scattered farms. Views over pastural stretch of Coquet Valley and village of Hepple.

31

Miles.	Places and route itinerary.	Information and Points of
2	**BICKERTON.** Continue to junc. B6341; here continue straight ahead to:	Farming hamlet on quiet byroad.
2.0	**SWINDON.** Turn R and follow byroad along west bank of River Coquet to:	Junction of B6341 to Elsdon. Wooded byroad alongside River Coquet.
2.5	**HOLYSTONE.** Continue ahead and in half-mile turn L; continue to:	PM. Picturesque small village to west of road; Lady's Well (NT) reached by field track at back of Salmon Inn. Parts of church are remains of 12 cent. nunnery. Well preserved Bastle House 1600.
2.0	**HARBOTTLE.** Continue ahead to:	EC: Wed. C (limited opening) Remains of motte and bailey on hill to east. Pleasant small village. Modern castle. Drake's Stone 1 mile west, views.
1.5	**ALWINTON.** (see note a) Turn L through village on narrow byroad; continue ahead and then descend steeply to:	B&B. PM. Cvg cmg. T (in car park) Church built on slope; ten steps between nave and chancel. The road continues for over ten miles through a narrow valley twisting and turning, crossing and recrossing the river.
2.0	**LINBRIGGS.** Cross bridge and turn R; continue on byroad and descend to:	Farm. Winding byroad. Places to picnic alongside river.
1.0	**SHILLMOOR.** Recross river and continue through valley to:	Farming hamlet on east bank of river.
3.0	**BARROWBURN.** Cross river again and follow river, in half-mile keep L and continue to:	Deserted hamlet. Small streams descend from the Cheviots to join the Coquet.
4.0	**BLINDBURN.** Continue to:	Isolated farm within two miles of Scottish border.

Miles	Places and route itinerary.	Information and Points of Interest.
1.0	FULHOPE. Climb steeply then continue to:	Farm. Here the Coquet is little more than a stream.
1.0	MACKENDON. At War Dept. barrier, retrace route through valley, return to:	End of public highway. (See note a and b) 1m west is site of Chew Green Roman Camp, complex of forts and camps Roman Dere Street. Pennine Way. Scottish border half-mile. Very easy ride on return to ALWINTON.
11.0	ALWINTON. In half-mile cross bridge (River Alwin) and immediately turn L; on byroad (see note d); climb for one-mile and continue to:	Optional diversiion to CENNELL (hamlet in secluded valley).
5.0	NETHERTON. Turn R through village and in half-mile again turn R; climb steeply then continue through:	Small village. Equestrian centre.
2.0	HIGH TREWITT. Descend for two miles through:	Farming hamlet.
2.0	SNITTER. In one-mile at T junc. turn R through.	Pretty small village .
1.0	THROPTON. At T junc. turn L (B6341) and continue into:	See Ride No.5.
1.5	ROTHURY.	See Ride No.5.

NOTES:
(a) The mileage to ALWINTON and return is 26. The extension of the ride through the UPPER COQUET VALLEY is optional and can be reversed at any point.
(b) When firing is not taking place, it is possible to continue beyond MACKENDON to BYRNESS.
(c) From ALWINTON, there is an alternative route back to ROTHBURY via HARBOTTLE, SHARPERTON, FLOTTERTON and THROPTON (See map). Distance approx. the same.
(d) From ALWINTON, there is an optional extension of the ride to CLENNELL, a hamlet in the picturesque ALWIN valley (two miles return).

Ride No. 7
From Bellingham:
Keilder Water and Forest - 43 miles

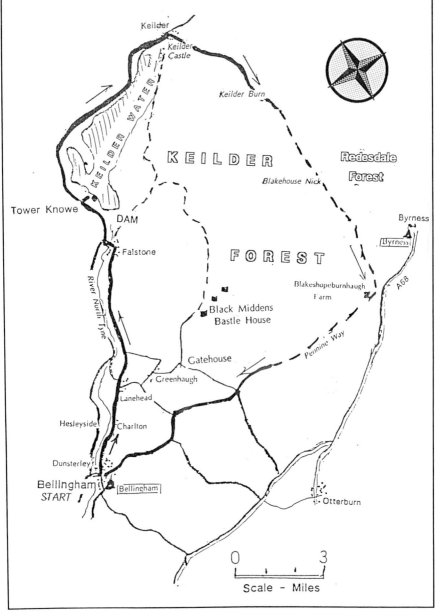

Keilder

Keilder Castle

Keilder Burn

KEILDER

Blakehouse Nick

Redesdale Forest

Tower Knowe

DAM

Byrness

Byrness

Falstone

FOREST

River North Tyne

Blakeshopeburnhaugh Farm

A68

Black Middens Bastle House

Gatehouse

Pennine Way

Greenhaugh

Lanehead

Hesleyside   Charlton

Dunsterley

Bellingham   [Bellingham]
START

Otterburn

KEILDER WATER

0   3

Scale - Miles

Ride No. 7
FROM BELLINGHAM: KEILDER WATER & FOREST. - 43 Miles.

The most interesting ride from BELLINGHAM is through the valley of the North Tyne and alongside the KEILDER RESERVOIR, the largest man-made lake in Europe surrounded by the largest Forestry Commission forest in England. The ride starts along an exciting byroad and then crosses to the south side of the valley and turns along the 'new' road alongside the Reservoir. At KEILDER village the route turns through KEILDER FOREST along a badly surfaced Forest Drive which is a Toll Road for motor vehicles. The final section back to BELLINGHAM starts along part of the PENNINE WAY and after another section of forest drive and two miles of rough track which is mostly rideable, it reaches a minor road and crosses open moorland before descending to BELLINGHAM. For riders who do not feel inclined to tackle the longer ride, a return might be made from KEILDER along a forest drive down the 'back' of KEILDER WATER returning to BELLINGHAM along the Bastle House Trail and Grenhaugh rejoining the outward route at Lane Head. (See note a and map)

Gradients: The first few miles are undulating with a few steeper climbs. The ride alongside KEILDER WATER is more gentle. There are several strenuous climbs on the Forest drive from KEILDER. After that the gradients are easier.
MAP: Ordnance Survey Landranger Sheet No.80.

Miles.	Places and route itinerary.	Information and Points of Interest.
	BELLINGHAM. From centre of village, take B6320 west when main road turns left; continue straight ahead on byroad; continue through:	EC: Thurs. Inf. B&B. YH: see page 66. Sh. C. Cmg. Cvg. Small market town. Church: St. Cuthbert's 13 cent. has stone vaulted roof, 12 cent. font. Pedlar's Pack grave stone. 17 cent coaching inn. Old houses. Bridge - River North Tyne. Hareshaw Inn, deep wooded dene with waterfall at head, 1.5 miles.
2.5	CHARLTON. Continue ahead to cross roads at:	Small farming hamlet.

Miles.	Places and route itinerary.	Information and Points of
1.5	LANEHEAD. Continue ahead and descend, cross bridge and climb for Half-mile then turn L; descend on field road and pass over disused level crossing; climb and then descend to:	New diversion to T junc. where turn right and then left.

This is a delightful gated lane route relatively free of traffic. |
5.0	FALSTONE. Turn L and descend to bridge (River North Tyne); climb to T junc and turn R; climb past south side of:	PM. C. Sh. Small village below Keilder Dam.
1.5	KEILDER DAM. Continue ahead along south side of reservoir and turn right to:	Inf. C. Cvg Cmg. Cyc. CH. Extensive views across KEILDER WATER. Built 1975.80.
0.7	TOWER KOWE Visitors Centre. Return to road and turn right; continue north to:	Inf. Cafe. T. Cycle Hire. On small peninsula in reservoir.
8.0	KEILDER VILLAGE. Turn R and cross bridge (River North Tyne) to:	PM. Sh. a Forestry Commission village built in 1950's The viaduct of the old Border Counties railway opened in 1862 is preserved but is not accessible.
1.0	KEILDER CASTLE. Continue ahead through forest (see notes a and b) and in 2m bear R and descend to bridge; then climb on FOREST DRIVE; climb for 2m on poorly surfaced road and then descend and again climb to summit at:	Inf. Cafe. Cycle Hire. The castle a former shooting lodge of the Duke of Northumberland is now an Information Centre and local social Club.
6.5	BLAKEHOUSE NICK. Descend and continue through wooded valley to:	Highest point on forest drive.

Miles	Places and route itinerary.	Information and Points of Interest.
5.0	**END OF FOREST DRIVE.** Turn R on Forest Road near Blakeshopeburnhaugh Farmhouse; Surface deteriorates as route ascends to:	Byrness: Cafe. Youth Hostel, 2m W. along A68. Next section of route follows part of Pennine Way (see map).
3.0	**GATE.** Continue on unsurfaced track across open moor and through private forest for 1.5 miles then continue on surfaced byroad; descend and in 1.5m after short climb, turn L and then turn R; continue on narrow byroad; in 2.5m bear L; in further 1m at T junc. (B6320) turn right descend into:	Here leave Forest. Good surface on this section. Gated. Wild open moorland.
9.5	**BELLINGHAM.**	

NOTES:

(a) As an alternative and shorter return to BELLINGHAM, turn left after bridge through Butteryhaugh and follow forestry road on left, mostly unsurfaced alongside RESERVOIR. There are a few steeper hills and several rough sections but all of it can be ridden. Follow red colour coded arrows to HAWKHOPE at end of DAM and rejoin the outward route at FALSTONE. Total distance by this route - 37 miles.

(b) Another alternative is by the Bastle House Trail. Follow above route (a) for six miles from KEILDER village at T junc of roads immediately beyond bridge over large burn (Belling Burn) with a ruin nearby (on right), fork left and climb steeply above the burn for almost a mile; continue on main forest road for nearly five miles to the public road at Target Burn. Half-mile further there is a public information board explaining Bastle Houses where a footpath to Black Middens Bastle (preserved by English Heritage) goes off. Continue on byroad to GATEHOUSE where there are two Bastle Houses (in private use). At next junc. turn right and at next T junc. turn left through GREENHOUGH; continue to LANEHEAD and turn left rejoining outward route.

Ride No. 8
From Bellingham:
Elsdon and Wallington Hall

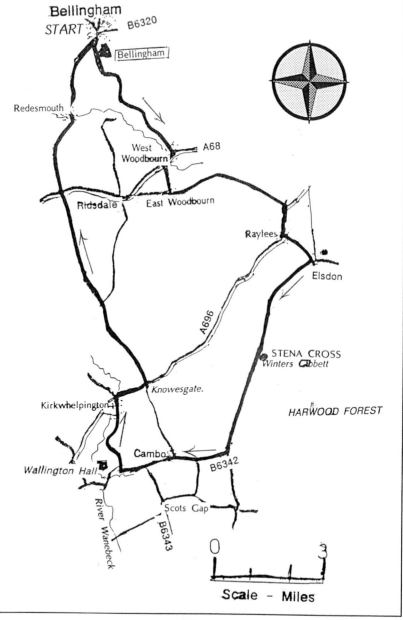

Bellingham
START
B6320

Bellingham

Redesmouth

West Woodbourn
A68

Ridsdale
East Woodbourn

Raylees

Elsdon

A696

STENA CROSS
Winters Gibbett

HARWOOD FOREST

Knowesgate.

Kirkwhelpington

Cambo

Wallington Hall
B6342

River Wanebeck

Scots Gap

B6343

0

Scale - Miles

Ride No. 8
FROM BELLINGHAM: ELSDON and WALLINGTON HALL - 35 Miles.

This route follows some byroads through open country to the east of BELLINGHAM. It passes through few villages and whilst not having any dramatic scenery, there are few main roads. There are however some extensive views. It is excellent cycling countryside ideal for a weekend or holiday time when the more popular places tend to be overcrowded. WALLINGTON HALL (National Trust) is a grand mansion in splendid wooded grounds.

GRADIENTS - For the most part the route is undulating starting with a climb out of BELLINGHAM. There is another climb out of EAST WOODBURN; a steep descent into ELSDON and a steep climb out of the village to the summit of Battle Hill. The return from KIRKWHELPINGTON is undulating ending with a steep descent at Redesmouth, two miles from BELLINGHAM.

MAP: Ordnance Survey Sheets 80 and 81.

Miles.	Places and route itinerary.	Information and Points of Interest.
	BELLINGHAM. From centre of village, climb hill past Youth Hostel; continue ahead passing HOLE and then descend to T junc. (A68) at:	See Ride No.7. Pele Tower. Extensive views over Redesdale; typical Northumberland countryside.
4.5	**WEST WOODBURN.** Turn R across bridge (River Rede) and in 150 yds turn L on byroad to:	Small village on one of main routes to Scotland formerly Roman 'Dere Street'. Site of Roman Fort, south of village built to guard Dere Street at crossing of River Rede. A substantial ruin appears to be a Border Tower but is in fact the engine house of a blast furnace of the Redesdale Ironworks, 19 cent.

Miles.	Places and route itinerary.	Information and Points of
1.0	**EAST WOODBURN.** Turn L and climb for one-mile then continue on gated road across open common; cross bridge (Raylees Burn) and climb to T junc. A696); turn R and in less than one-mile at:	Picturesque hamlet in Rede valley. Wild countryside. Extensive views.
4.5	**RAYLEES.** Turn L (short stiff climb) and in half-mile descend steeply into:	Farming hamlet on busy Newcastle Carter Bar road.
1.5	**ELSDON.** Retrace route for 150 yds and fork L; climb steeply and then continue climbing up BATTLE HILL to:	PM. Sh. C. T. Cvg. Cmg. (2 miles north at Billsmoor Foot). Once a busy place, capital of Redesdale now a quiet village built around a green with a church in the middle. Motte and Bailey of Norman castle to north. Tower overlooking green is a well preserved 14 cent pele which became the Vicar's Pele. Now much altered and is a private house.
2.5	**STENG CROSS.** Continue ahead across open moor and in 3.5m at junc. with B6342, turn R; continue to:	Altitude 312 metres. Winter's Gibbett, modern replacement with replica wooden head on the gibbett on which William Winter was hung in 1791 for a murder at a farmhouse.
6.0	**CAMBO.** Continue ahead to:	Attractive village associated with Wallington Hall Estate. School was attended by 'Capability' Brown, the Landscape Gardener.
1.0	**WALLINGTON HALL.** Retrace route for half-mile and turn L on byroad to:	Inf. NT. Gardens. Youth Hostel in stables for 25 years (1931-55). House built in 1688 and altered later, of honey coloured stone in plain classical style. Surrounded by beautiful gardens, woods, lakes, walled flower garden and ornamental bridge over River Wansbeck.

Miles	Places and route itinerary.	Information and Points of Interest.
2.5	**KIRKWHELPINGTON.** Continue to T junc. (A696) and turn R; in one-mile at:	Small village set back from A696. T. On edge of moors. River Wansbeck. Church - St. Battholemews. memorial to Sir Charles Parsons inventor of steam turbine.
1.0	**KNOWESGATE Cross Roads.** Turn L on byroad and keep left in 2.5 miles passing SWEETHOPE LOUGH; continue to cross roads (Junc A68); continue straight ahead and in half-mile fork R then descend into:	Cafe.

Lough in moorland setting.

Extensive views. |
| **9.5** | **REDESMOUTH.** Cross bridge (River Rede) and continue into: | Small village in sheltered valley where River Rede joins North Tyne. Once a railway junction. |
| **2.0** | **BELLINGHAM.** | |

The byroad from EAST WOODBOURN to ELSDON is typical of the open country in this part of Northumberland.

Ride No. 9
From Bellingham:
Wark Forest & Roman Wall - 43.5 miles

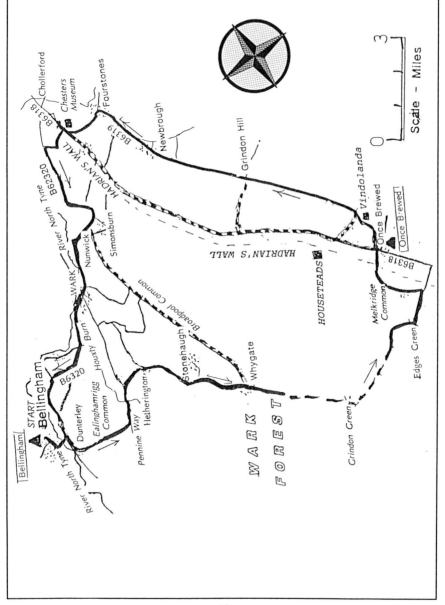

Ride No.9
From BELLINGHAM: WARK FOREST & ROMAN WALL.
- 43.5 Miles.

This is a fairly strenuous ride which includes several miles of off-highway riding through Wark Forest but it is a really excellent cycling route through remote countryside away from the usual tourist traffic. There is an opportunity to visit the Roman Fort at Vindolanda and the Chesters Fort and Museum which contain 'finds' from the Roman occupation of the area. The fort of Housesteads on the Roman Wall may also be visited by making a detour from Vindolanda although this involves riding along the Military Road the B6318 for 2.5 miles which is frequently busy with traffic. Alternatively the Youth Hostel at Twice Brewed might be used as a base for the latter part of the route which is concentrated on the Roman Wall and the various forts and museums.

Gradients: There are several climbs but none of them too strenuous. The first is from Dunterley on leaving the valley of the North Tyne. The climb through WARK FOREST is well graded but there is a steep climb from Melkridge Common to the crossing of HADRIAN'S WALL. The return ride from Chesters through WARK involves one steep climb after WARK.

MAPS.- Ordnance Survey Landranger Sheets No. 80 and 87.

Miles.	Places and route itinerary.	Information and Points of Interest.
	BELLINGHAM. From centre of village, take B6320; cross bridge (River North Tyne) and in 200 yds turn R on byroad to:	See Ride No.7.
1	**DUNTERLEY.** Turn L on byroad and climb; in half-mile turn L; climb steeply and continue across EALINGHAMRIGG COMMON; at T junc turn L; descend and cross bridge (Houxty Burn) turn R on field road; climb steeply and turn R past:	Farming hamlet on byroad to KEILDER. Quiet road. Pennine Way follows part of this road.

Miles.	Places and route itinerary.	Information and Points of
4.0	**HETHERINGTON FARM.** Continue through open country passing turning for:	C at Honeystead farm (on L of route).
3.0	**STONEHAUGH.** Continue straight ahead to:	Forestry village. Cmg. Cvg. Picnic site.
1.5	**WHYGATE.** (see note a). Continue ahead and climb then continue through forest; on badly surfaced forest road; continue on grassy track to:	Last settlement before entering WARK FOREST. See Note a.
3.0	**GRINDON GREEN.** (Ruined farm) in further half-mile, turn L and cross footbridge at side of ford; continue along track (gated) at side of forest then continue on open byroad to:	Grass grown track from here. May be difficult in bad weaher but excellent off-highway route in good conditions.
3.5	**EDGES GREEN.** In one-mile 200 yds after telephone kiosk, turn L on byroad across MELKRIDGE COMMON then climb steeply to HADRIAN'S WALL; continue to staggered cross roads at:	Farm in remote location behind HADRIAN'S WALL. Steel Rigg (Car Park on left) is a good place from which to visit HADRIAN'S WALL. Eastwards is an exciting walk of one-mile to CRAG LOUGH. Half-mile westwards is Winshields, the highest point on the Wall.
3.0	**ONCE BREWED.** Cross over (B6318) on byroad; descend and then turn left on narrow byroad (Stane Street) for one-mile to:	National Park Visitors Centre. Inf. Twice Brewed YH. B&B. PM. Cmg.
1.5	**VINDOLANDA.** Continue downhill on Stanegate here unsurfaced; pass entrance to Chesterholm and climb to T junc. turn L and in half-mile turn R; (see note b) continue ahead and descend to:	Roman Fort on Stanegate which precluded HADRIAN'S WALL. Large civilian settlement which has been extensively excavated. MUSEUM at Chesterholme House east of fort. Note Roman Milestone in its original position beside burn. Still on Stanegate

Miles	Places and route itinerary.	Information and Points of Interest.
		pass Grindon Lough cross roads at Grindon Hill and Settingstones. Splendid views of Tyne Valley and Houseteads Camp.
3.0	**NEWBROUGH.** In half-mile continue ahead on B6319 through:	T. Pleasant village in wooded setting where byroads descend into South Tyne Valley.
1.0	**FOURSTONES.** Climb then continue ahead; at T junc (B6318) turn R to:	Village on B6319 where this turns away from River South Tyne.
2.5	**CHESTERS HOUSE & FORT.** Turn L into byroad opposite MUSEUM; in half-mile turn R and at X rds (junc B6320) turn L then take third road on L uphill; turn right at T junc over bridge into:	House not usually open to public. Visit to FORT and MUSEUM strongly recommended. Finds from Roman occupation. Site slopes down to River North Tyne. Well preserved Roman Bath House and abutment of bridge which carried the Wall over the river. (best seen from east side of river) (footpath from Chollerford Bridge (see map).
4.0	**SIMONSBURN.** Turn right in village and descend to bridge (Red Burn); turn left to rejoin B6320 at:	Small attractive village on Crook Burn. 18 cent cottages. Handsome church from 13 cent. Impressive Geogian rectory.
0.5	**NUNWICK.** Continue to:	Small estate village. 18 cent. house. not visible from highway.
2.5	**WARK.** Turn L and immediately turn R (sp B6320 Bellingham); descend to bridge (Houxty Burn); climb steeply then continue ahead descend and cross bridge (River North Tyne); continue into:	EC: Thurs. B&B. Sh. T. Large village of grey stone cottages around pleasant green with trees. Once capital of Tynedale. Bridge 1878 over River Tyne.
5.5	**BELLINGHAM.**	

NOTES:

(a) For a shorter route and to avoid the off-highway ride through WARK FOREST, turn left at WHYGATE and cross Broadpool Common then descend to T junc (B63220) where rejoin main route at NUNWICK. Detour to SIMONSBURN recommended (See map).

(b) For HOUSETEADS FORT, continue fromCHESTERHOLM to T junc. with B6318; turn R for one-mile. Entrance through Car Park on L. Fort is half-mile walk up hill on good path. The main route can be rejoined by continuing ahead for further 1.5 miles and then turning R to Grindon Hill. (See map).

Ride No. 10
From Haltwhistle:
South Tyne Valley and West Allendale
- 28.5 miles

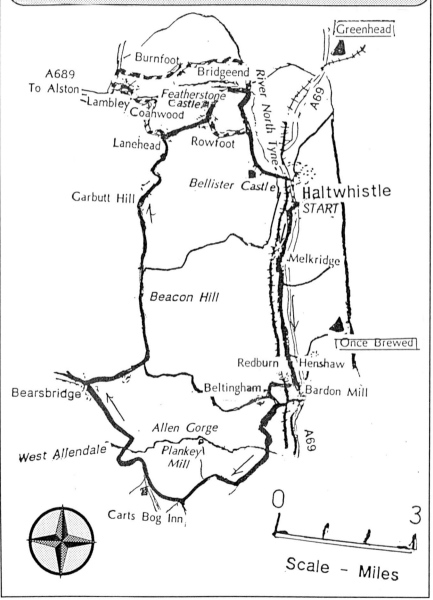

Ride No. 10
From HALTWHISTLE: SOUTH TYNE VALLEY and WEST ALLENDALE.
- 28.5 Miles.

This route first follows a byroad - formerly the A69 - through the valley of the south Tyne after which there is a strong recommended diversion into the picturesque village of BELTINGHAM. After a climb to Carts Bog Inn the route descends into the valley of West Allendale. There is then a climb through hilly country before returning to the South Tyne at Rowfoot. Apart from a few miles on the A686 when this descends from Cart Bogg Inn into West Allendale, the route avoids main roads so is ideal for a weekend or holiday time.

GRADIENTS - This is a hilly route. The first few miles from HALTWHISTLE are easy but then there is a strenuous climb to the Cart Bog Inn after which there is a steep descent into the Allendale valley. There is another climb from BEARSBRIDGE to BEACON HILL and a steep descent into the South Tyne Valley at Featherstone Castle.

MAP - Ordnance Survey Landranger Sheet No. 87

Miles.	Places and route itinerary.	Information and Points of Interest.
	HALTWHISTLE. From town centre, descend to T junc. (A69); turn L and in 50 yds turn R on to 'old A59' continue ahead through:	EC: Wed. MD; Thurs. Inf. BR. Sh. Cafe. T. Small town centre now by-passed by A69. YHs at GREENHEAD (3m NW) and ONCE BREWED (3m NE).
2.0	**MELKRIDGE.** Continue ahead through:	Small village now bypassed by A69.
2.0	**REDBURN.** Continue ahead to T junc. (A69); turn R and descend into:	Quiet almost deserted byroad Join main road for 1.5 miles.
0.5	**BARDON MILL.** Continue ahead and in 300 yds (after road to railway station) turn R on track which descends to level crossing; continue to foot bridge over River South Tyne; turn L on byroad to:	BR. PM. C. Cmg. Sh. Village formerly on busy A69 but now bypassed.

Miles.	Places and route itinerary.	Information and Points of
1.0	**BELTINGHAM.** Continue through village to T junc; turn sharp L and then sharp R imm. before railway bridge and bear L (see note a); in 400 yds descend to bridge (River Allen) climb very steeply at times for 1.5 miles turn R and descend to T junc. (A686); turn R past:	Picturesque hamlet in North Tyne valley. Allen Banks (NT Picnic area. T. Allen Gorge Pict. Walks by River. Allen to Plankey Mill in mature woodland. Plankey Mill on byroad to R. Access to walks.
5.0	**CARTS BOG INN.** Continue ahead and descend very steeply (sharp bends) to bridge (River Allen); continue through valley of River West Allen to:	PM. Isolated Inn on A686 Penrith-Hexham tran-Pennine road. Cmg. Cvg. Care required on three sharp bends. Picturesque wooded valley. Waters meet where Rivers East and West Allen join.
4.0	**BEARSBRIDGE.** Turn R on byroad and climb steeply and continue to T junc. and turn L to summit of:	Sh. Hamlet beside picturesque bridge. Ahead along the A686 is Whitfield Hall and church and scattered estate village in pleasant wooded valley of West Allen.
1.5	**BEACON HILL.** Continue to:	Wild exposed country but fine views.
4.5	**GARBUTT HILL.** At X rds continue ahead and bend sharp L; climb for half-mile and at T junc. turn R; continue straight ahead to cross roads at:	Farming hamlet.
1.5	**LANEHEAD.** (See note a) Turn R and descend steeply to cross roads at:	Hamlet.
1.0	**ROWFOOT.** At T junc. turn L across disused level crossing and descend steeply past:	PM. Hamlet.

48

Miles	Places and route itinerary.	Information and Points of Interest.
0.5	**FEATHERSONE CASTLE.** At foot of descent, turn R alongside River South Tyne to:	<u>Care required on steep descent.</u> Beautifully situated 'fairy tale' castle in wooded valley. Remains of 13 cent. house and 14 cent. tower built into early 19 cent. house in castellated style. Short walk by the river to R goes to former Prisoner of War camp where German officers were held brick buildings remain.
1.5	**BRIDGE END.** Continue ahead and climb steeply for 400 yds; pass first turning and turn L over footbridge (old road bridge) under railway bridge and directly over A69 into.	18 cent single span bridge rises steeply from road junction. Cmg Cvg. Bellister Castle on R remains of Pele tower and 13 cent house. (NT). Adjoining house 17-19 cent.
2.5	**HALTWHISTLE.**	

NOTES.
(a) Alternative route from LANEHEAD; Continue straight ahead through COANWOOD and descend to bridge across River South Tyne; continue through LAMBLEY and at T junc. (A689) turn R; after short climb turn R on byroad; after short descent continue through BURNFOOT; turn L and climb steeply; descend steeply and cross bridge at BRIDGE END. Here join main route.
(b) From BRIDGE END there is a direct route to GREENHEAD Youth Hostel (see map).

The picturesque village of CRASTER, famous for its oak smoked kippers.

49

Ride No. 11
From Ninebanks:
Allendale Town and Coalcleugh - 25 miles

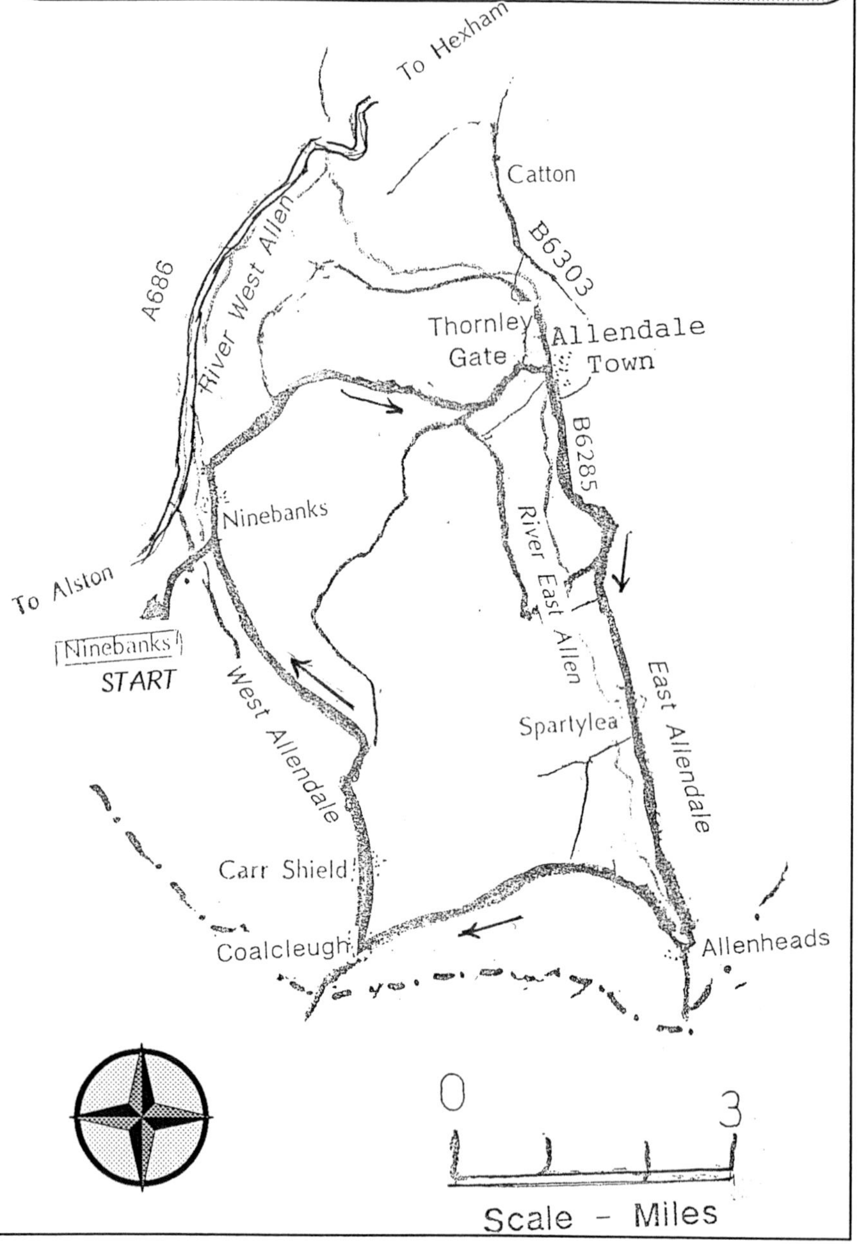

To Hexham

Catton

B6303

A686

River West Allen

Thornley Gate

Allendale Town

B6285

Ninebanks

River East Allen

To Alston

Ninebanks START

West Allendale

Spartylea

East Allendale

Carr Shield

Coalcleugh

Allenheads

0 3

Scale - Miles

Ride No. 11
From NINEBANKS:
ALLENDALE TOWN
and COALCLEUGH.
- 25 Miles.

This ride provides for a leisurely exploration of the twin valleys of East and West Allendale. The main centre for the area is Allendale Town although it is no more than a large village. It stands on high ground above the River East Allen and has a broad square surrounded by stone houses and hotels. It is famous for an annual ceremony on New Year's Eve when barrels of blazing tar are carried to a bonfire in the market place. This area of the North Pennines was extensively mined for lead from Roman times. The ruins visible on the moors and in the valleys are 18 and 19 cent. workings with crushing and smelting mills and long flues running up the hillside to tall chimneys which are a prominent feature of many skylines. This is another ride which would be suitable for a holiday period.

GRADIENTS: Variable - most of the climbs and descents are when moving from one valley to the other and vice versa. Riding up and down the two valleys is relatively easy.

MAPS: Ordnance Survey Landranger Sheet No. 87.

Miles.	Places and route itinerary.	Information and Points of Interest.
	NINEBANKS Youth Hostel. From Youth Hostel, descend to T Junc. continue ahead and cross bridge (River West Allen); turn sharp L and continue ahead through:	Cottage Youth Hostel (see page 67) in isolated location on eastern slopes of Pennines.
1.5	**NINEBANKS Village.** In half-mile turn R; climb very steeply for 1.5 miles then continue ahead and descend to:	Hamlet alongside River West Allen. Open country extensive views.
4.0	**THORNLEY GATE.** Turn R on major road; cross bridge (River East Allen) and	Small farming village in valley of East Allen. A smelt mill with an underground flue almost 2 1/2 miles long with prominent chimneys still visible on the moors.

Miles.	Places and route itinerary.	Information and Points of
1.0	**ALLENDALE TOWN.** Turn R in square (B6295) and continue through East Allen valley, climbing steadily through:	EC: Wed. B&B Sh. Cafe. T. Compact stone built village in a well wooded location. Bonfire festival held each New Year's Eve when Guizers carry blazing tar barrels on thir heads to a bonfire in the market place, a custom that dates back to the pagan past. Once the centre of an important lead mining industry which finally collapsed in the 1920's. Now a popular tourist centre. Church. sundial.
5.5	**SPARTLEA.** Continue ahead to:	Hamlet in upper East Allen Dale. Old Lead mining centre. YH at First Pot. 1949-72.
2.5	**ALLENHEADS.** Turn R past Inn and continue alongside river; in 1m turn L and climb for 2.5m then descend to:	Cafe. PM. T. Small village at head of dale surrounded by high moors and desolate remains of lead workings.
4.0	**COALCLEUGH.** Turn R and descend steeply at times through:	Another old lead mining village in moorland setting at head of West Allendale. Now almost deserted.
1.5	**CARR SHIELD.** In half-mile turn L and continue through valley and alongside river; immediately past NINEBANKS church; turn sharp L; cross bridge and climb steeply to:	Straggling hamlet above West Allen. River. Remains of lead mining buildings mostly ruins.
5.0	**NINEBANKS Youth Hostel.**	

The road to Ninebanks Youth Hostel turns across a bridge over the West Allen River.

The ruins of the Roman Camp at CHESTER extend to the banks of the River North Tyne (Ride No.9).

53

Ride No. 12
From Hexham:
Blanchland and Derwent Reservoir
- 31 miles

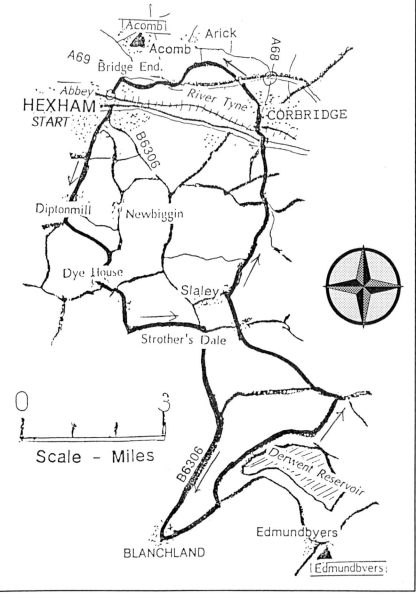

Ride No. 12
From HEXHAM:
BLANCHLAND and
DERWENT RESER-
VOIR - 31 Miles.

In the hilly country to the south of HEXHAM, are several small villages hidden in wooded valleys and linked together by a network of quiet byroads. After wandering along some of these byways, the route eventually leads to the ancient village of BLANCHLAND, a beautiful spot on the Durham border. The return ride follows the north shore of the Derwent Reservoir and then climbs through woodland before descending into the Tyne valley.

GRADIENTS - The ride is a succession of climbs and descents but none of the climbs are really strenuous.

MAP - Ordnance Survey Landranger Sheet No. 87.

Miles.	Places and route itinerary.	Information and Points of Interest.
	HEXHAM. From town centre, leave by Eastgate (B6306) and after passing hospital turn R (sp Racecourse); climb for one-mile and at X rds continue straight ahead, descend steeply to:	EC: Thurs. MD: Tues. Inf. BR. Cvg. Cafes. Sh. B&B. YH: at Acomb 2m NW. Ancient market town on a rise above the River Tyne. Now a busy shopping and commercial centre capital of Tynedale. Priory church 12-13 cent. founded on site of 7 cent church of St. Wildred's the crypt of which built with Roman stones survives. Cross in market place. Formidable 15 cent moot hall leads to 14 cent prison. Several ancient streets lead off Market Place. Variety of 17 and 18 cent houses.
2.0	**DIPTONMILL.** Climb for half-mile and turn L (sp Dye House); in 1.5 miles, at T junc turn R and descend to:	Hamlet in wooded valley.
3.0	**DYE HOUSE.** Cross bridge; climb to T junc and turn L; descend and after short climb turn R on byroad to:	Small village in valley.

55

Miles.	Places and route itinerary.	Information and Points of
1.5	**DUKESFIELD.** Continue ahead around bend and over two minor cross roads:	Farming hamlet on northern edge of Slaley Forest. Smelt Mill 18 cent now a substantial ruin. Lead ore was once brought here by pack horses for melting.
2.0	**STROTHERS DALE.** Turn R (B6306) (sp Blanchland); continue ahead and descend into:	
4.5	**BLANCHLAND.** Turn L at church into square on B6306; cross over bridge into County Durham and in one-mile turn L to recross River Derwent back into Northumberland; continue along north shore of:	EC: Thurs. Sh. Cafe. Pm. Unspoiled village of stone built cottages. Built from remains of 12 and 13 cent monastery. The church was the chancel of the monastic church. Lord Crewe Arms is a picturesque mixture of monastic and 18 cent gothic. The village square is on the site of the outer court and is entered by a 15 cent gatehouse, a mixture of medieval and 18 cent stonework.
4.0	**DERWENT RESERVOIR.** Turn L and climb to X rds; turn L and in half-mile fork R; continue through forest to outskirts of:	Huge expanse of water, 3 miles long built in 1960s, has transformed the valley. Picnic sites. Pleasant byroad through forest. Ahead are the grounds of the Ministeracres Monastry. Cycling is permitted through the grounds.
5.0	**SLALEY.** Turn R and in 2m descend into valley and at foot of hill, turn L on narrow byroad; in 400 yds fork R and climb steeply; at X roads continue straight ahead and descend steeply (sharp bends) to T junc. (A695); turn L and imm. turn R (sp Corbridge); cross railway bridge and at TR, turn R and cross narrow bridge with TL (River Tyne) into:	PM. Centre of Village to L. Care on descent. 17 cent bridge is oldest over River Tyne. All the others were swept away in great flood in 1771.

Miles	Places and route itinerary.	Information and Points of Interest.
5.0	**CORBRIDGE.** In centre of town, turn L to Market Place and then turn L on side street; half-mile from town pass under bridge (A69 Dual Carriageway); continue ahead and in 2m cross bridge (A69); descend to:	EC: Thurs. Inf. B&B. PM. Cafes. T. Sh. Cmg. Cvg. Attractive small stone built town described as the jewel of the Tyne Valley, now an expanding residential area. It was once the capital of Northumbria. The church has a Saxon tower and much earlier fabricated Roman features reused from Corstopitum. The Vicar's Pele, 14 cent restored at side of church. Roman town of Corstopitum (half-mile west) founded as a fort guarding Dere Street, became a garrison town in the 3 cent. Interesting museum on site.
3.5	**BRIDGE END.** At T junc. turn L and cross bridge (River Tyne) into:	Suburb of HEXHAM. Industrial site. Tyne Green Riverside Park on right.
0.5	**HEXHAM.**	

The charming village of Blanchland. Ride No.12

Ride No. 13
From Hexham:
Tyne Valley and Military Road - 28.5 miles

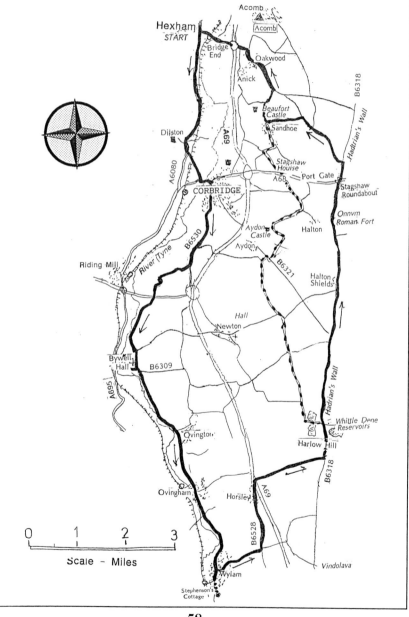

Ride No. 13
From HEXHAM:
TYNE VALLEY and
MILITARY ROAD.
- 28.5 Miles.

The first part of this ride keeps close company with the River Tyne as it approaches Tyneside. From CORBRIDGE, it follows a quiet byroad to WYLAM after which it turns north away from the river and climbs to HADRIAN'S WALL although this stretch is not so spectacular as the parts of the wall further west. Parts of the route might conveniently be used to or from NEWCASTLE-upon TYNE and other parts of TYNESIDE, eg. cyclists arriving at NEWCASTLE-upon-TYNE to begin a tour of Northumberland.

GRADIENTS - From HEXHAM to WYLAM, the gradients are very easy but there are a few climbs from WYLAM to HADRIAN'S WALL after which there are many easy descents.

MAPS - Ordnance Survey Landranger Sheets 87 and 88

Miles.	Places and route itinerary.	Information and Points of Interest.
	HEXHAM. From Town Centre, leave eastwards by Woodlands and continue along A695 to:	See Ride No.12
2.5	**DILSTON.** Just past the turn into the village fork L; at TR turn L and cross bridge into:	No village but remains of 14 cent. tower and house with fragments of Dilston Hall once the 17 cent. house of the Earls of Derwentwater in grounds of modern Hall. Basle House but no access to public.
1.0	**CORBRIDGE.** At cross roads in centre of town, turn R on B6530 (old A69); in 2m turn R on byroad; descend to side of River Tyne and continue to:	See Ride No.12. Quiet byroad which closely follows River Tyne.

Miles.	Places and route itinerary.	Information and Points of
5.0	**BYWELL** At cross roads, turn R into village then retrace route to X rds; turn R on B6309 and imm. fork L on byroad alongside River Tyne; in 2m at T junc. turn R into:	Claimed to be the most beautifully placed architecturally interesting group of buildings in the Tyne valley. Two Saxon churches beside each other, late 17 cent. old vicarage. Market Cross. Castle is a big gate house. Tower of 15 cent. is now part of a private house. Large landscaped grounds of Bywell Hall. There is no village as such. It was swept away for landscaping and the villagers moved to Stocksfield on the south side of the Tyne. St. Andrews has the best Saxon tower in the county but St. Peter's retains a more ancient fabric.
3.0	**OVINGHAM.** Continue ahead alongside river to:	B&B. PM. sh. Pleasant village above River Tyne. St. Mary's church has late Saxon tower. and Saxon stonework remains in a mostly 13 cent church. 18 cent. packhorse bridge. 15 cent Inn. Thomas Bewick the engraver is buried in the churchyard.
2.5	**WYLAM.** At entrance to village turn L; climb for 1.5m to X rds (B6528); turn L through:	BR. B&B. PM. Cafe. T. Pleasant residential village on north bank of River Tyne. Birthplace in 1781 of George Stephenson father of the railways. His birthplace half-mile east (open by arrangement). The cottage then faced directly on to a wagonway. This is now a public track for cyclists beside the River Tyne. Wylam Station opened in 1835, one of the earliest stations still in use. Railway Museum.
2.0	**HORSLEY.** In half-mile turn R under bridge (A69); continue ahead to:	Small village now bypassed by A69.
2.0	**HARLOW HILL.** Turn L (B6318); in one-mile at X rds (B6309) continue straight ahead (see note a) to TR at:	Small village on 18 cent. military road B6318 was partly constructed on remains of Hadrian's Wall which was levelled to provide a firm foundation. The Ditch and Vallum of the Roman Wall are very clear on part of this section. Reservoirs (1848-50) at Whittle Dene provide water to Newcastle.

Miles	Places and route itinerary.	Information and Points of Interest.
5.5	**STAGSHAW ROUNDABOUT.** Continue ahead for half-mile and then turn L on byroad through open fields and at X roads continue ahead and then turn L; descend into outskirts of:	PM. Port Gate. Crossing of A68 road to Scotland. Roman Dere Street passed through Hadrian's Wall at the gate. Care when negotiation TR. Traffic very heavy. Quiet and attractive byways on route back to HEXHAM which avoid main roads.
2.5	**SANDHOE.** Turn R and then right again continue ahead past OAKWOOD; and descend steeply to TR at A69; continue staight ahead through BRIDGE END; cross bridge (River Tyne) into:	Small village in woodland on steep flank of Tyne Valley. Several attractive houses.
3.0	**HEXHAM.**	

NOTE.
(a) From WHITTLE DENE RESERVOIRS, there is an alternative route to SANDHOE. At cross roads, turn left on B6309; in half- mile at Welton Farm. Continue straight ahead for 3 miles to T junc. with B6321; turn R and in a few yards turn L pass road to AYDON CASTLE, (13 cent. EH.) on L at right hand bend; in nearly one-mile turn L and continue to T junc with A68 (opposite Stagshaw House); turn L and then turn R (busy road take extreme care when turning); turn R at cross roads and climb steeply into SANDHOE. Turn L to rejoin main route. Scenically the Military Road is preferable.

On Ride No.4. there is an optional diversion to the picturesque village of Rock.

Ride No. 14
From Morpeth:
Belsay and Netherwitton - 37 miles

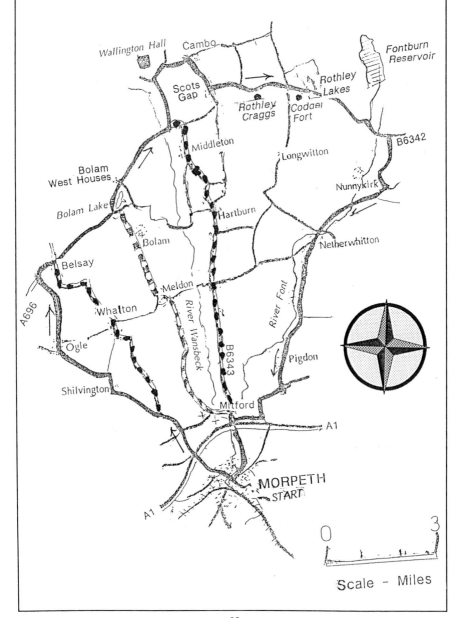

Scale - Miles

Ride No. 14
From MORPETH:
BELSAY and
NETHERWITTON.
- 37 Miles.

To the west of MORPETH, after crossing the A1 Great North Road, there is a web of byways which link together some small villages and after passing Bolam Lake Country Park, lead to WALLINGTON HALL (see Ride No. 8). On the return, there are more traffic free byways making this an ideal ride for beginners or riding with children. The route might be used a 'link route' between MORPETH and the rides in the BELLINGHAM and ROTHBURY areas.

GRADIENTS - There are few climbs. For the most part the routes follow the WANSBECK and FONT valleys so gradients are gently undulating.

MAPS - Ordnance Survey Landranger Sheets 81 and 88.

Miles.	Places and route itinerary.	Information and Points of Interest.
	MORPETH. From town centre, cross bridge (River Wansbeck) (A197) and climb past park below castle; at TR keep to R and in one-mile turn R (B6524); continue past Golf Course and pass under bridge (A1 By-pass); take third turn L for 1.5 miles to:	EC: Thurs. MD: Wed. Inf. BR. B&B. Sh. Cafes. County town of Northumberland since 1974. Busy expanding town. Remains of castle in hill south of River Wansbeck, now a private house. St. Mary's church - 14 cent. Bridge chantry 13 cent. much altered and now restored. Inf. Centre. Bridge on A197 by Telford 1830. Clock Tower belfry in middle of Oldgate probably 17 cent. using older masonry. Town Hall in market place by Vanburgh, 1714. Court house, now hotel has massive heavy gateway to former gaol, on L south of bridge.
5.0	**SHILVINGTON (Farm)** In half-mile bear L and continue to:	No village, merely a country road junction.
2.5	**OGLE.** Continue ahead through village and then bear L; in 1.5 miles at T junc. turn L to T junc (A696); turn R into:	Small village with long street. Castle is mostly 16 cent. well restored.

Miles.	Places and route itinerary.	Information and Points of
2.0	**BELSAY.** Continue through village and at junc with B6524, fork R on byroad, and in 2m keep L past:	Cafe. Sh. T. Small estate village on A696 Newcastle-Carter Bar Road. One-mile through estate to Castle. Entrance to Belsay Hall and Park. Large wooded grounds and gardens surround early 19 cent. house in style of Grecian Temple. Walk through quarry garden to 14 cent. tower house and early 17 cent. manor house now roofless.
2.5	**BOLAM LAKE.** Continue ahead and in 2.5 miles after crossing bridge (River Wansbeck), turn L; in one-mile at T junc (B6342), turn R to:	Attractive and popular Country Park. T. Cafe at Bolam West Houses one-mile beyond lake.
4.5	**WALLINGTON HALL.** Continue ahead through:	NT. inf. See Ride No.8.
1.0	**CAMBO.** Beyond centre of village, turn R (B6343) to:	18 cent. model village on Wallington Estate. Attractive cottages in cluster off through road. Capability Brown famous landscape gardener went to school here. Post Office was once a Vicar's Peel Tower.
1.0	**SCOTS GAP.** Turn L on minor road; cross bridge (Hart Burn); climb and then pass ROTHLEY CRAGS (on right); continue to:	Small village with cattle market and former railway junction. National Trust Regional Office. Part of Wallington Estate landscaped in 18 cent. ROTHLEY CASTLE is a Gothic folly built as an eye catcher and viewpoint on top of the crags.

Miles	Places and route itinerary.	Information and Points of Interest.
2.5	**ROTHLEY CROSS ROADS.** Continue straight ahead (B6342) across ROTHLEY LAKE; climb then descend and cross bridge (River Font); climb for half-mile then turn R on byroad; in 1.5m at T junc. turn R; in 1.5 m cross bridge (River Font) and continue into:	Codger Fort is another Gothic folly on craggy hillside north of cross roads. ROTHLEY LAKES are picturesque fishing lakes created by Capability Brown on both sides of the road, half-mile north of cross roads. For Fontburn Reservoir 1904, (1m west) turn off before Font Bridge on narrow private road.
7.0	**NETHERWITTON.** Turn L across bridge (Rive Font) and continue ahead for 2m; bear L and then turn R; continue through:	Small village in valley of River Font. Hall has late 17 cent front and 16 cent back.
4.0	**PIGDON.** At T junc. in half-mile, turn R and in 1.5m at Cross roads on approach to A1 junction, turn R; descend steep hill to confluence of Rivers Font and Wansbeck on approach to:	Small farming hamlet.
3.0	**MITFORD.** At T junc. (B6343) turn L; pass under bridge (A1 Bypass); in one-mile sharp double bend over narrow bridge (care required) continue to T junc. A192 (old A1) turn R into:	PM. SH. Recommended detour to small village on R over Font Bridge, 1.5 miles return. Turn L on B6343 then turn L on byroad; descend and cross bridge (narrow and on bend); Ruins of Castle on hill ahead. Church dates from 12 cent but looks 19 cent. Old Manor House in ruins near church has porch tower. 17 cent. Road continues south to give fine views of Mitford Hall, 19 cent. in spacious grounds.
2.0	**MORPETH Town Centre.**	

NOTES:
(a) Between MORPETH and BOLAM LAKE there are alternative routes (see map)
(i) Via Whalton (PM. Sh. T) a picturesque village with tree lined main street.
(ii) Via Meldon and Bolam (Halland church).

(b) From WALLINGTON, there is a more direct route to return to MORPETH via MIDDLETON AND HARTBURN.

Youth Hostels Profiles.

WOOLER (Cheviot).

WOOLER, the most northerly of England's Youth Hostels, is only a few miles from the Scottish border. During the 1939-45 war, the building was a Womens Land Army Hostel. It was taken over by the YHA in 1974 although there had been a previous hostel at Wooler from 1932 in the old railway station. That had been closed in 1940 so the present hostel was a welcome replacement.

It is located on a byroad which climbs above the small town so is easy of access. It has 57 beds and although it is a simple grade hostel, meals are available. It is ideally situated for use as a base by cyclists who wish to tour in the northern corner of Northumberland following the first three rides in this guide or as a 'link hostel' when heading for the Borders region of Scotland.

BELLINGHAM.

BELLINGHAM Hostel, a wooden building on a hill above the small town was one of the first hostels to be specially built for the purpose. It was opened in 1936 and been in constant use since that year. It is very popular with cyclists as it is convenient for a wide choice of routes in the Upper Tyne Valley and in more recent times for visiting Keilder Water. It also is ideally located for an overnight for cyclists bound for the Scottish Lowlands via Keilder.

The hostel is closed from November to the end of February. Weekly closing night is Sunday. It has 34 beds and although meals are not provided there is a well equipped kitchen for self catering. There are shops in the town (half-mile) and also some cafes.

One feature which has been retained is a solid fuel burning stove in the centre of the Common Room around which members gather on cold evenings to yarn about their activities.

GREENHEAD.

The hostel at GREENHEAD is near to the county's western boundary and within half-mile of the Roman Wall.

It has 40 beds and is housed in a former Methodist Chapel. First opened in 1979 so by comparison with other hostels in this area, is comparatively new. Meals are supplied. The nearest town is Haltwhistle (two miles), which is the starting point for Ride No.10.

ONCE BREWED.

Seven miles from GREENHEAD, along the Military Road, is another Hostel at Once Brewed. The total accommodation is 76 which includes some Family Rooms. This is the best situated hostel for visiting HADRIAN'S WALL; and the various forts and the museums at HOUSTEADS and CHESTERS. It is also on the route of Ride No.9 where this emerges from WARK FOREST so the ride might conveniently be ridden from there as an alternative to BELLINGHAM.

Meals are supplied and there is a store carrying a stock of essentials food for Self caterers.

ACOMB.

Acomb is another hostel with a history going back to 1933. It is situated in the main street of the village and was converted from stable buildings. There are beds for 40 and although meals are not provided, there is a store at the hostel supplying essential foods. It is only open at weekends in the winter and has a weekly closing night - Mondays - in the summer.

The hostel is only two miles away from the busy town of HEXHAM so it is ideally situated for Rides No.12 and 13 (See route maps). The Roman Museum at Chesters is less than five miles away so Ride No.9 could also be picked up from Acomb.

NINEBANKS.

Ninebanks Hostel is hidden away in the hamlet of Mohope in West Allendale on the eastern slopes of the Pennines. It has provided Simple Grade accommodation for those cyclists and walkers who delight in discovering out of the way places since 1946.

The primitive building was formerly a lead miner's cottage but it has been made into a really cosy hostel. Meals are not supplied but there is a small store.

It is a convenient base for Ride No.11 but might also be considered as an overnight halt for cyclists making a cross Pennine journey between Northumberland and the Lake District as it lies a short distance off the A686 road to Alston.

When cycling along the coast road north from Seahouses, there is a fine view of Bamburgh Castle. Ride No. 3.

Warkworth has an impressive medieval castle which rises above the village on the banks of the River Coquet. Ride No. 4.

CYCLING AROUND Series.

This is one of a series of guides researched and prepared by Arnold Robinson, at one time the Cyclists' Touring Clubs Local Touring Adviser for Derbyshire and the Peak District..

They have been designed to assist cyclists, especially beginners, who are planning a cycle tour or cycle rides in the area. So far as is practicable, the routes follow quiet little used backroads - and occasionally off-highway routes - to avoid the heavy traffic which is often experienced on the main roads in the Peak District at weekends and holiday times.

Apart from the itineraries for the suggested cycling routes, details are given about road surfaces and gradients; places of interest; viewpoints and scenic attractions; touring information including the location of Bed and Breakfast accommodation; Youth Hostels, Camping Barns, Camp Sites, Shops, Cycle Hire Facilities, Toilets etc., and most important for cyclists, the whereabouts of Cafes and other places to eat.

The route maps indicate the suggested routes and when used in conjunction with the itineraries should be adequate for following the route. Details are also given of other maps for the area which will assist in identifying other routes if variations are made from the suggested tour.

There are more than twenty CYCLING around guides - see separate list.

The guides can be obtained from many Tourist Information Offices, at some cafes and at local shops or direct from the publishers.

© Arnold Robinson 1997.

CYCLING GUIDES
by ARNOLD ROBINSON.

All contain Route Itineraries, Route Maps, details of Gradients and Surfaces, Touring Information, Points of Interest, Viewpoints and Scenic Attractions, Location of accommodation, Youth Hostels, camp sites, places to eat and cycle repairers. The suggested cycling routes may be ridden as 'day rides' or linked together to form an on-going tour.

CYCLING Around CASTLETON and the Hope Valley.

CYCLING Around MATLOCK.

CYCLING Around BUXTON

CYCLING Around CHESTERFIELD.

CYCLING Around LEICESTERSHIRE & RUTLAND

CYCLING Around LINCOLNSHIRE.

CYCLING Around NORTHUMBERLAND

CYCLING Around THE LAKE DISTRICT.

CYCLING Around the NORTH YORKSHIRE MOORS - ten routes which provide an on-going tour.

CYCLING Around STAFFORDSHIRE

CYCLING Around the COTSWOLDS

CYCLING Around the YORKSHIRE WOLDS.

CYCLING Around DERBY

CYCLING Around THE ISLE OF MAN

CYCLING around the PEAK DISTRICT - contains eleven routes which may be ridden individually or linked together to form an 'on-going' tour. Details are also given of the popular off-highway Trails.

CYCLING around SHEFFIELD - nine routes in Sheffield's 'Golden Frame.'

CYCLING around HARTINGTON -touring information and route itineraries.

CYCLING around BAKEWELL - touring information and route itineraries.

CYCLING around ASHBOURNE - touring information and route itineraries.

 CYCLING in DERBYSHIRE - eleven of the best cycling routes, mainly in the southern half of the country.

CYCLING in NOTTINGHAMSHIRE - twelve cycling routes which cover most of the county.

CYCLING around CHESHIRE - twelve routes.